HELPLINE
TEEN ISSUES AND ANSWERS ™

WHEN A FRIEND OR LOVED ONE DIES

GRIEVING, MOURNING, AND HEALING

ALEXANDRA HANSON-HARDING

ROSEN
PUBLISHING®
New York

To my father, Robert Eldon Hanson Sr., my "other parents,"
Harry and Kaye Harding, and Marge Springer

Published in 2014 by The Rosen Publishing Group, Inc.
29 East 21st Street, New York, NY 10010

First Edition

Library of Congress Cataloging-in-Publication Data

Hanson-Harding, Alexandra.
When a friend or loved one dies: grieving, mourning, and healing
/Alexandra Hanson-Harding.—First Edition.
    pages cm.—(Helpline: teen issues and answers)
Includes bibliographical references and index.
ISBN 978-1-4488-9447-5 (library binding)
1. Teenagers and death. 2. Bereavement—Psychological aspects. I. Title.
BF724.3.D43H36 2014
155.9'370835—dc23

2012045526

Manufactured in the United States of America

CPSIA Compliance Information: Batch #S13YA: For further information, contact Rosen Publishing, New York, New York, at 1-800-237-9932.

CONTENTS

In the Hanson family, there is a one-hundred-year-old photograph. It shows the great-grandparents Steen and Christiana Hanson and their twelve children in their North Dakota home. This portrait looks odd to modern eyes. It isn't just the formal clothes and strict postures. It's also because one of the children isn't there. Instead, a portrait of a small blonde girl is held by two other children. Like so many families in that era, these parents had lost a child. But although she was gone, she wasn't forgotten. The portrait showed that she was still part of the family.

In 2007, actress Bella Thorne's father was killed in a motorcycle accident. Bella was nine. "Saying good-bye to my daddy was one of the hardest things I've ever had to do," she told *M Magazine*. She continued, "Sometimes I'm afraid I'll forget what he looked like or what the sound of his voice was like. We have pictures all over our house, but it's a different feeling to be able to close my eyes and really see him. That's the feeling I'm afraid to lose."

Her longing echoes the feeling of many grieving people. When someone you love dies, for him or her, there is no future. But for you, there is—a future without that person. Small shocks come again and again. You text your friend, but he can't answer. You're hungry for your mom's cookies, but only she knew the recipe. Your brother's winter coat is still in the closet, but he'll never see snow again.

In 1850, Alfred Lord Tennyson wrote his poem "In Memoriam" to his best friend, who died at the age of

Actress Bella Thorne lost her dad, but he continues to inspire her. She is pictured here at a Valentine's Day celebrity party a couple of years after her father's death.

twenty-two. Tennyson's grief was so powerful, it took him seventeen years to write it. In it, he wrote, "Tis better to have loved and lost / Than never to have loved at all." That sounds awfully noble. But if you lose your best friend, and the pain won't let you sleep, is it really lucky to have loved and needed your best friend so much? The pain can be so intense that you wish you could feel it all at once, have one session of utter misery and never feel it again. But that is not how it usually works. Grief takes time—but its course may move back and forth in unpredictable patterns of varying moods.

As Dr. Eileen Kennedy-Moore, a therapist from Princeton, New Jersey, told the *Record* newspaper, "You don't have to go through stages in a certain order. You can do the stages backward, skip stages, invent your own stages. There is no right way to grieve."

Eventually, the death of a loved one can sometimes lead to a new kind of growth. In fact, for Bella Thorne, her father's words inspired her: "My favorite quote is one he used to say: 'Persistence breaks resistance.' He taught us to never give up." After her father's death, Bella truly focused on acting. "I hope my daddy can see how much my family's done," Bella said.

On December 18, 2012, Newtown, Connecticut, was forced to come to terms with loss in a more violent way. A gunman entered Sandy Hook Elementary School and murdered twenty children and six staff members. The world joined in sympathy, mourning for the young victims and the brave teachers who tried to shelter them.

Readers will meet other people who have lost loved ones. You will learn how they cope, what to expect, how they grieved, and how they reentered the world with new insight and awareness.

The Beginning After the Ending

More than 2,450,000 million people died in the United States in 2010, according to the Centers for Disease Control and Prevention. For each person who dies, many more people are affected. If you are reading this, chances are that either you or someone else you care about is struggling with death.

FORGOTTEN MOURNERS

Young people used to be what some people call "the forgotten mourners." They were kept away from funerals and often told as few details as possible. Instead of saying that the person died, adults would use unclear phrases such as "passed on" or "in a better place." But now, many experts believe that kids and teens can often handle death better if they are included in traditions such as funerals, especially if they are prepared beforehand. Facing death head-on can help young people develop their coping skills.

In Newtown, Connecticut, mourners attend a candlelight vigil on December 15, 2012, after twenty-six children and staff members were murdered at the town's Sandy Hook Elementary School. The gunman also shot his mother and himself, bringing the death toll to twenty-eight.

WHAT HAPPENS AFTER A DEATH?

After people die, their bodies, or remains, are left behind. Different cultures have their own traditions about what happens to the remains. Some people are buried in coffins. Others are cremated, or burned to ashes. Others donate their bodies to science. Sometimes bodies are missing or are buried in a faraway land. But even in those cases, there is often some kind of memorial service to mark the person's death.

How Can You Prepare Yourself for a Funeral?

Before you go to a funeral, you might want to prepare with these tips:

- Drink some water and eat something before the service so that you won't be distracted by thirst or hunger.

- Dress respectfully.

- Bring tissues, cough drops or mints (not gum), and maybe a small object to hold (maybe something that reminds you of your loved one, like a watch or a locket, or even a smooth stone) to ground yourself.

- Turn off your cell phone.

- Volunteer to babysit a younger sibling or cousin if you want distraction for a little while.

- Try to be open-minded about what you will experience. You may find that it is not only bearable but also meaningful to be there.

- If you feel overwhelmed, find a quiet place until the funeral is over. But if you feel like crying, go ahead. Crying is normal at funerals.

- If there is a pamphlet of the service, make sure you keep a copy. You may want to look at it later.

However you end up handling the emotions of the service, remember that this is a difficult time. Have mercy on yourself and on the other people who share in the suffering of the death of your loved one.

WHY ARE FUNERALS AND MEMORIAL SERVICES IMPORTANT?

Some people say that funerals are "for the living." There is something deeply human about recognizing the passage of life into death. Ever since ancient times, human remains have been buried with care. Memorials are a ritual of transition. They show the reality that the loved one is gone and give others a chance to honor the person's life.

WHAT HAPPENS AT A FUNERAL?

In some cultures, there is a wake a day or two beforehand to say good-bye. Often wakes are open-casket, meaning that visitors can see the person's body. It can be hard to see a loved one who is no longer breathing. But it can help viewers understand that the person has died.

During a funeral, the coffin is usually at the front of the room. A clergy person may lead prayers and say a sermon. People may share some memories. There may be music, perhaps including a song the person loved. In some traditions, there is also a graveside service.

Often there is a gathering with food afterward. People talk, sometimes laughing and often sharing memories of the person who died. Many people find comfort in eating and socializing with friends and relatives that they may not see very often.

If you are asked to share memories, you can be humorous if you are kind. Here, a teen shares memories of a murdered friend.

SHOULD YOU SPEAK AT THE FUNERAL?

You may be asked to participate in the funeral in some way. You could sing a song, read a poem, or tell a story about your lost loved one. Your story can be humorous, but it should always be kind. This is not the time to complain or be bitter. When seventeen-year-old Terrence's father died, his parents were divorced and his father had broken many promises to come see him and his sister. Yet his father had many friends at the funeral. Terrence looked around and said, "I'm happy that so many people loved my Dad." Later he was proud he had found a way to be truthful but kind.

GOING BACK TO REGULAR LIFE

When you first learn that a friend or loved one has died, it can be a great shock. You may just want to sit in a chair playing a computer game or stare blankly out the window. But funerals are busy times. People can make a fuss over you. Soon, however, they return to their normal lives while you are still suffering. Students have to go back to their regular lives, too.

GOING BACK TO SCHOOL

Returning to school can be intimidating after someone you love dies. According to an interview that teen Ashlyn

The school library can be a haven for a grieving teen who needs a place to retreat. It can also be a good place to find resources to help with mourning.

McCain gave to CNN, the first day she went back to school after her father's funeral, "I walked down the hallway and all I heard was people whispering, 'That's the girl whose dad died.' 'That's the girl whose dad got killed,'" she said.

Before you go back, think of "safe places." That means, places where you can retreat, such as the library or the guidance office. You can ask your parent or guardian to write you a note to excuse you from class when you feel too upset, for example. Then you can go to your safe place for a little while until you gain control of yourself. Ask if there is a support group for people at your school. Think, too, of adults you would feel safe talking to, such as a guidance counselor, teacher, or librarian.

Julie Goldberg is a teacher and a librarian in New Jersey. As a librarian, she sometimes encounters grieving teens looking for a quiet, safe place. What does she do to help? "I just listen to whatever [grieving teens] want to tell me." She added, "It's important teachers know what has happened, and maybe even some detail so they don't mistake normal grieving behavior for being disengaged or noncompliant."

CONCENTRATING ON SCHOOLWORK

Even if you're a good student, it may not be very easy to concentrate on schoolwork when you've lost someone. You can experience many intrusive thoughts that can make you miss what's going on in the classroom. If you find that happening to you, you might want to get a study buddy who will share his or her notes or remind you of what you missed—especially your homework assignments. As difficult as it may be, the more you can stay on top of your schoolwork, the better off you will be. If you work at it, even slowly, you may find that you become so interested in it that it takes your mind off your other troubles. For young people, the most important job they have is being students—it has a direct effect on their future.

Keeping busy with activities, including shopping, can help take your mind off your grief.

In dealing with grief, you may have to try more than one approach at a time to give yourself a happy life. Goldberg says, "I think that it is good for grieving people to throw themselves into more than one kind of activity, not just schoolwork, which can be isolating, but, as much as possible, into social activities, sports, extracurriculars, etc. Or some manageable combination. It's not good for grieving people to be alone too much."

THEY MEAN WELL

When you lose someone, people can act weird. Some people say the wrong things:

- "It could have been a lot worse—at least she died quickly."
- "You'll have to be the man of the family now."
- "I know how you must feel because my dog died."
- "You have to move on now."
- "There's no point to grieving—you're just feeling sorry for yourself."
- "You should be grateful because she's in a better place now."

When well-meaning people say hurtful things, it's a double whammy. First, you're angry about what they said. Then you're feeling guilty because they are trying to be helpful—they just aren't. Actually, it can sometimes feel as if people aren't really thinking about you at all; they're just trying not to feel scared of the same thing happening to them.

They also might start asking more questions than you're comfortable with answering. You have a right to say "That's enough," or "I don't really want to discuss it now." Tell as little or as much as you want—be the gatekeeper. Nobody is entitled to the "gory details."

Even worse, some people may stay away from you because your tragedy can represent bad luck to them. Or when they do talk, they're more interested in giving advice and sharing their own examples of suffering than in listening to yours. This may be even worse with adults, who may not know how to talk to young people. But you may not want your grief to be compared to someone else's sad story. You may not want their advice. You may just want to be listened to. You may want to tell your story over and over again. Talking about your loved one—or even grieving about him or her—can feel like a way of keeping the person alive.

Fifteen-year-old Hannah Tjaden from Killeen, Texas, said of her soldier dad, who died in January 2009, "I try to tell a lot of people about it. I want people to know about him." She told CNN, "They just look at me weird. They don't really listen."

So how do you get friends to listen? One way is just by being direct. Step back and frame your thoughts. Think—*why does that bother me?* Then say calmly, "I don't think you understand how I feel," and explain why. Or you can say, "I really need someone to talk to about Lara. You don't have to say anything, I just need a few minutes to say how I feel."

If you are sincere, you might help them understand what you need from them and how you feel. If they don't, try not to let their foolishness make you bitter. Good friends can help you get through the worst times. If you can have compassion for their clumsy efforts, and listen to them, too, you may be able to reconnect to a healthy life more quickly.

The Grieving Process

In 1969, Dr. Elizabeth Kubler-Ross introduced the idea of the five stages of grieving based on the feelings of the dying patients she studied. According to Kubler-Ross, the five stages of grief are: 1) denial; 2) anger; 3) bargaining; 4) depression; and 5) acceptance.

Unfortunately, many people have overgeneralized her work. They have applied her ideas in ways she did not originally mean. Some assumed that each step would rigidly follow the last. Moreover, they assumed that the feelings of people who grieve for someone who dies are the same as the feelings that someone would feel about his or her own death. When experts or others became too rigid in their following of Kubler-Ross's ideas, they got across the idea that to grieve any other way is "unnatural."

Actually, all of these emotional responses are common for mourning people to feel. But grief is deeply individual and has its own pace and rhythm. For some, it can be short; for others, it can take longer. It can flare up again at holidays, or stressful times, yet allow for periods of less pain as well.

SOME TYPICAL SIGNS OF GRIEF FOR ADOLESCENTS

However, acute grieving *is* common after a loss takes place. It wouldn't be surprising to have some of the following common, difficult grieving experiences.

RUMINATION

One excruciating feeling some mourners feel is a pattern of obsessive thoughts, called rumination. Teens might have the same images, questions, and ideas repeat themselves: Why do other people have their mothers and I don't? Who will die next? If God is so powerful, then why didn't He save her? What happens to the spirit of the person who died? One of the few ways to break through rumination is by distracting yourself with positive activities. But if ruminating thoughts last all day for months, you may need to look for help.

ISOLATION

Grieving can feel like being behind a glass wall. You may feel as if others can see you, but not hear you. They are the normal people now. You used to be one of them, but now it's different. You can't believe they can complain so angrily about bad traffic, a nasty teacher, or a pimple. *Really?* That's what they worry about when you lost someone you loved? Their concerns can seem so trivial, it's hard to relate to them. You may need private time—but you might also want to seek out a support group if you are too lonely.

Many grieving teens need time alone to process the death of a loved one. Some people experience physical pain or are unable to sleep when they are mourning.

HALLUCINATIONS AND DREAMS

Many people actually experience hallucinations, or visions, of the person they lost after the loved one's death. These can occur when the griever is awake. Grievers also commonly have dreams about the person who died. These sensations can be both a comfort and a curse. Bella Thorne still has these dreams, according to *M Magazine*. "I do dream about him," she says of her father. " I know he's watching over me."

After a seventeen-year-old classmate drowned, Valerie Benkol had nightmares about him for almost a year. As she said in *Chicken Soup for the Soul: Tough Times for Teens*, "I had a recurring nightmare for close to a year after Keith's death. In it, I was standing by the river and he was walking toward the water. I kept yelling for him to stop, not to enter the water, but he always did. One night, the dream was different. After I yelled for him to stop, he turned to me and smiled saying, 'It's OK. I'm alright.' Then he disappeared into the dark water."

PAIN

People who are grieving may often have physical pain. That is, they don't just feel the pain in their heads; they also feel it in their bodies. They get headaches, feel exhausted and weak, feel strange aches and pains in their arms and legs, or have stomachaches. Often they also can't sleep.

ANGER

You may find yourself wanting to do something destructive, especially if you feel as if your grief is being ignored. Instead of asking for the help they need, some teens engage in risky behaviors such as smoking, drinking, or taking illegal drugs. This often backfires because it makes the teen seem less sympathetic and more like a problem than someone who needs to be heard. The rapper 50 Cent, whose mother was murdered when he was a boy, became a bully and engaged in other harmful behaviors that he later regretted.

THE GOOD NEWS ABOUT GRIEVING

New research is showing that grieving is a difficult but normal process and most people are psychologically prepared to handle it. According to Ruth Davis Konigsburg, author of *The Truth About Grief: The Myth of Its Five Stages and the New Science of Loss*, many people handle grief better than they thought they would. "Loss is forever, but acute grief is not, a distinction that frequently gets blurred," she said.

Dr. George Bonanno, author of *Good Grief: Coping After Loss*, conducted a study about married people who'd lost their spouses. He inquired if the living spouses had been in happy or unhappy marriages. To his surprise, he found that there was little relationship between the quality of the marriages of the subjects and those who recovered quickly or slowly. In fact, he discovered that for

Complicated Grief

Some people don't cope so well, however. When their grief is prolonged and serious, it is called complicated grief. Often it involves depression. Depression is different from grief. A healthy grieving person is often aware that he or she is going through a process and that things will change. But someone who is suffering from complicated grief may feel unrelenting suffering or emptiness for days or months on end. The individual may believe his or her sadness is permanent. If people suffer from complicated grief, they may need psychiatric medications and therapy. Support groups can be a good place to start as well.

the most part, people who grieved for shorter periods weren't just pushing the memories of their spouses out of their heads. Instead, they were finding happiness in the memories that they and their loved ones had shared. One reason why is that they used their inner strength to find ways to cope with death. How?

UNDERSTANDING THAT EMOTIONS ARE REAL, BUT THEY CHANGE

Experiencing something as serious as death can make you realize one of the greatest truths in life: you can have all kinds of feelings—including reactions that are surprisingly not sad—even at the darkest moments. Your cat might jump into the sink and make you laugh, or you might still want to go to a party and dance.

Even in the midst of grief, it's OK to take time to have fun. Don't feel ashamed for wishing to do your usual social activities.

Don't feel guilty for feeling happy or wanting to live your regular life. The length of anyone's life is a mystery. Everyone will die—you just as much as anyone else. If you were to die tomorrow, wouldn't you want people you loved to appreciate and enjoy their lives?

SOMETIMES, DEATH CAN BE A RELIEF

Some people have self-destructive behavior that is frightening to be around, such as taking drugs or drinking too much. Some parents are even abusive toward their families. Oscar-winning actress Charlize Theron was fifteen when her alcoholic father came home and threatened her with a gun. Her mother shot him dead. Her mother was never charged with the shooting. As sorry as she was to lose her father, at least Theron knew she and her mother were safe.

YOU CAN HELP OTHERS

Through experiencing the death of a friend or loved one, you learn skills that can help others. You have knowledge, such as how to get through a funeral and grieving. You have a better idea about how to help people who are suffering and what to say—and not to say. You know that life does not last forever and it's serious. Your sufferings also enhance your claim to be a legitimate spokesperson for causes that matter, both to you and the person you lost.

PRACTICING LIVING IN THE MOMENT

Another finding of Dr. Bonanno was that, sometimes, repressing and avoiding the feeling of grieving—whether by distracting yourself with tasks or focusing on something positive—can speed recovery. He checked his subjects six months and fourteen months after their losses. He found that people who could do these things without denying the gravity of the loss were both mentally and physically healthier than those who didn't.

Actor Jon Hamm has won Emmy Awards for his role on the TV show *Mad Men*. But his life has been tough. His mom died when he was ten, and his dad when he was twenty. "Losing both parents at a young age gave me a sense that you can't really control life—so you'd better live it while it's here," Hamm told *Parade* magazine. "I stopped believing in a storybook existence a long time ago. All you can do is push in a direction and see what comes of it."

Liz Murray would agree. Her drug-addict mom died of AIDS when she was fifteen. Her dad died a few years later. But even though she was left homeless, she over-came her upbringing to graduate from Harvard University. How did she come to terms with the deaths of her unreli-able but loving parents?

"Tragedies serve as a reminder of what is very impor-tant in life," Murray told *Teen Voices* magazine. "When [my mom] died, I realized I did not have the 'later' that I thought I had." Writing her memoir, *Breaking Night* (2010), was "almost like being able to connect with them again...That took me up and down some very intense roller coasters of emotion that were very tough to deal with—but also in a way, a beautiful sadness," she continued. "Life changes," she said. "You can carve out a life for yourself that is not in any way limited by your past."

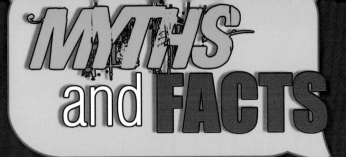

MYTH If you are grieving, you will always be sad.

FACT Grieving is a natural process. You will likely feel a variety of emotions as you go through it, including happiness and joy at certain moments.

MYTH If you don't feel sad, then you're not grieving and you are being disrespectful to your loved one.

FACT If you gave respect and care to the person in his or her lifetime, that is what matters. You can feel many different feelings toward the dead, and they can change often.

MYTH You will always be a broken person if you are suffering now.

FACT Even if you are suffering from complicated grief that lasts a long time, you can get help that can make you a healthier, stronger person and live a good life.

Different Losses

If you lose a family member, home may be different—in big and small ways—after a death. There's an empty place at the table, or maybe a generation that is gone. If you lose a friend, you may have complicated fears about your own mortality. Here are some of the effects of losing important people in your life.

DEATH OF A PARENT

Actress Rosie O'Donnell's mother died of cancer at the age of thirty-nine. Her mom's funeral took place on Rosie's eleventh birthday. Her grief-filled father got rid of most of his wife's possessions. But one thing he missed was her mom's record collection. So, when her father was out of the house, Rosie and her siblings would listen together to them. "When we came home from school, [my mother] would put on Barbra Streisand's *A Happening in Central*

Staying busy doing things with friends, like going to the movies, can be a healthy distraction from sorrow.

Park and cook dinner, and we would sing all the songs to it. [My father] didn't know about that, because that was a ritual that was done while he was at work . . . So the only thing I had that was hers were the records. My love of Barbra Streisand is totally taken from my mother," she explained to *Redbook*.

Death can have an ongoing effect on young people's lives—but its meaning changes over time. Occasions like

Father's Day, Mother's Day, or other holidays can be tough, including loved ones' birthdays. Those are a good time to find special new rituals. Many young people may find that special occasions such as graduations, award ceremonies, and proms may bring back the pain of missing their parents as well.

"My father didn't get to see me graduate from high school," seventeen-year-old Sonya told a bereavement group called the Dougy Center, in the book *Never the Same*, written by Donna Schuurman. "And he won't be around to give me away if I get married, and he'll never get to be a grandfather. My kids will never have that grandfather, and that makes me really sad." Your successes in life may make you wish your parent could have been around to celebrate with you.

WHAT'S TYPICAL?

Your parents aren't there to teach you. How do you learn what's normal? How do you know how to shave, tie a tie, or put on makeup? There are certain things that young people need advice about, especially from a same-sex parent. To fill in that gap, you may need to find other adult role models you trust. It could be a counselor, an uncle or aunt, or a family friend. Organizations like Big Brothers/Big Sisters also provide mentors for young people. But do reach out—there are many young

Talking to a trusted adult, especially one of your own gender, can help you learn some essential matters about growing up.

adults who would feel enriched by having a friendship and sharing helpful life advice with a younger person.

The singer Madonna lost her mother at age five. When her stepmother wanted her to watch her younger siblings, she was angry. "I really saw myself as the quintessential Cinderella," Madonna later said. Her grief for her mother made her not want to listen to her stepmother. "I think that's when I really thought about how I wanted to do something else." She rejected her family's values and became famous for her rebellious personality as well as her singing.

WHEN YOU HAVE NEW RESPONSIBILITIES

Although Madonna was unhappy at the expectations placed on her, not all young people are resentful about pitching in. If your father used to cut the lawn, who will do it now? If your mom has to work more hours, who will pick up the kids after school? You may be the one your little brother turns to with his questions. These responsibilities may be hard. But they may also benefit you in the future, just as learning any skill can help. Besides, it may take pressure off your parent so that he or she can have more attention available for you.

DEATH OF A SIBLING

When Elizabeth de Vita-Raeburn was fourteen, she lost her big brother, Ted, to a disease called aplastic anemia.

Afterward, people would say, "That must be terrible for your parents." Instead of feeling her own sorrow, she felt a special responsibility to make her parents' lives easier. When she started to go to therapy when she was twenty-six, she told her therapist, "I am my brother's death." She found herself having to rediscover a sadness she'd never been able to name until she was an adult. She wrote

Supportive parents or other relatives can help young people cope with the death of a sibling by reminding them that they, too, are important.

about it in a book entitled *The Empty Room: Surviving the Loss of a Brother or Sister at Any Age*.

When a brother or sister dies, parents can get obsessed with the tragedy. Sometimes they can be neglectful or overprotective. Like Elizabeth, you may end up feeling invisible. Or that it is now your job to make up for the other child's death by being perfect all the time. If this happens, you may want to sit down at a quiet moment with them and say, "Look, I know that things have been tough since Sarah died. But I still need you. I'm having my band performance on Tuesday and I'd really like you to be there." Letting them know they're important to you is healthy because it can help remind them that they are still needed.

You might not know how to answer the question, "So, do you have any brothers or sisters?"

D. B. Zane's brother, Chad, died when D. B. was sixteen years old. When asked that question, he felt so awkward that he would first avoid social situations. Then he would say that one brother was a junior and the other was dead. But, as he wrote in *Chicken Soup for the Soul, Just for Teenagers*, "My tone wasn't very kind . . . This was no way to make friends . . . The weight of carrying my brother in my heart grew lighter. And then one day it happened: Someone asked me, 'Do you have any siblings?' 'Two brothers,' I responded automatically. There was no hesitation . . . One of my brothers may no longer be of this earth, but he is part of my family of five forever."

DEATH OF A GRANDPARENT

Losing a grandparent is commonly a young person's experience of death. How you feel will depend on your relationship with your grandparent. It may seem more natural that a grandparent die than a parent because he or she is older. But if you are close with that grandparent, it is still very sad. Librarian Julie Goldberg said that her

Kids often have special relationships with their grandparents, so losing them can be difficult.

daughter, fifteen-year-old Grace, frequently called her grandmother when she was sad or had a problem. "Her Bubbe was her 'go to' person," Goldberg says. "That's what she lost." Even now, Grace frequently wears her stylish grandmother's clothes to school.

In some cases, grandparents do even more. According to Grandparents.com, the U.S. Census numbers for 2010 showed that nearly five million kids—about 7 percent of under-eighteen-year-olds—live with their grandparents. They point out that two recent presidents, Bill Clinton and Barack Obama, spent significant parts of their childhoods with their grandparents. In fact, President Obama was raised by his grandparents from age ten until he went to college.

DEATH OF A FRIEND

Having a friend die can be not only deeply sad but also confusing. Young people aren't supposed to die. Some have called it "grief out of season." Some teens are killed by accidents or other sudden catastrophes. But others get illnesses that last a long time.

If you care about your friend, helping him or her through a time of illness can be one of the hardest tests of character that you can face. It can be scary to see your friend lose her hair if she has cancer or accept that sometimes she's too weak to talk. It's hard to hang out in a hospital with all of its strange smells. You also both know that if your friend's disease is fatal that you will be the one left behind, unable to share another secret. But as hard as it is, there are good reasons to hang in there with a dying friend. There are few times in life when you can make more of a difference. Your presence will make your friend feel normal, even if all you do is play a computer game together or gossip about school. You can also learn about the value of life. Dig down and be your best self—because being with people who are close to death isn't just a chore. It's an honor, if you let it be. You might even find you suffer less if he or she dies than you might have if you had avoided your friend or cut him or her off.

10 Great Questions TO ASK A GUIDANCE COUNSELOR

1 How am I supposed to pretend everything is normal when I have experienced something that none of my friends can understand?

2 If I am feeling sad in class, is it better to try to hold it together and focus on the material or to honor my grief by leaving?

3 What should I do if I can't stop dreaming or having visions in the daytime about my lost loved one? Is that a dangerous sign, or is it OK?

4 What should I do if I feel I'm being burdened with too much extra child care, housework, or other chores since a parent died and it's interfering with my life?

5 How do I know when it's better to hide away and grieve or to get outside and kick a ball around or go shopping?

6 Am I an uncaring person if I completely forget to think about my loved one sometimes?

7 How will I know if my sadness means that I have complicated grief and need extra help, or if it's just normal?

8 My family is fighting over who should get what of my grandparents' possessions. Will I end up doing that with my siblings? What are some ways I could avoid that?

9 If my brother, sister, or parent committed suicide, does that mean I'm going to end up committing suicide, too, someday?

10 What are some ways I can use my experience of grieving to help other people?

Slow Deaths, Quick Deaths

Grieving can be difficult for those who lose someone slowly, but it's not easy to lose someone suddenly, either.

SLOW DEATHS

Watching someone you love suffer can be difficult. It can be painful and scary to see someone you love grow weak and deteriorate. Pain can make him or her short-tempered.

When your parents have to make a lot of medical decisions for dying relatives, it can be tough. They can face struggles about the right thing to do. They can face battles about the right treatment and hospitals, money, who will take care of the dying person, if the person should be in a nursing home, and who should inherit what. A parent's death can stir up complicated feelings—even between adult siblings. Their troubles may spill over to the children, too.

Another worry can be resources. When a lot of money is spent on expensive treatments, families can get into financial trouble. That stress can be distracting for parents and can leave kids feeling cheated of their own future opportunities. This situation can also mean that teens have to take on extra chores and responsibilities, like babysitting, cleaning, and cooking while parents are busy with caretaking duties. Sometimes this burden can be too much—especially if it prevents you from having time to do your schoolwork or activities that are important to you or seeing your friends. Then it's time to talk to your parents about finding a better balance if it is possible.

TIME TO PREPARE

On the other hand, slower deaths sometimes let everyone prepare for what is to come. If the person you are losing is from an older generation, you can feel that you have nothing to offer, but that is wrong. The fresh, lively spirit of young people can be most encouraging and positive to someone who is dying.

Sometimes sharing the experience, the final passing can be sad and yet meaningful. Bill used to rub his

Babysitting younger sisters and brothers can build closer relationships and give assistance to your family, but you may still need time for yourself.

grandma's feet when she was in the nursing home. She loved his stories of school, and he loved her stories of growing up. After she died, he was surprised when his mother told him how much he had meant to his grandmother (and even more surprised at what it meant to him).

One good thing people can do is to listen. This period is a good time to write down memories or record them on a video camera. Often older people or dying people have things they want to say. They want their memories to count. They want to be remembered. They might want to give advice to their children and grandchildren for the future. This moment is the time to gather their wisdom.

Even being with loved ones at the very end of their lives can be meaningful. Grace Springer-Goldberg and her brother, Isaac, stayed with their grandmother through her last hours, singing to her quietly as she slept before she slipped away.

SUDDEN DEATH

Sometimes people die unexpectedly of heart attacks or other medical conditions. Some are killed in unexpected tragedies, such as the terrorist attacks of 9/11. But according to the *American Journal of Public Health*, the top five causes of injury death are 1) suicide; 2) car crashes; 3) poisoning (mostly by prescription drugs); 4) falls; and 5) murder.

With any kind of sudden death, a feeling that something very unnatural has happened can pervade people's

Calming Your Amygdala

The amygdala is the part of your brain that deals with emotional memories and strong feelings. It triggers fight-or-flight behaviors when there is a threat. People who have suffered trauma are easily stressed even when there is no current danger. Teaching your brain not to react when there is no emergency calms the amygdala and lets the brain think and plan again. If you are doing a puzzle or laughing at something on TV, then there must be no reason to feel as if you have to fight a bear! Learning to soothe your amygdala helps you tolerate tough experiences without making the emotions grow larger. How? When you feel danger, exercise may help. When you feel sad, chatting with a friend, snuggling with a cat, or taking a bath may work better.

feelings. So can the feeling that there is something you could have done to stop the death. It can be very easy to think, "If only . . . ," such as, "If only she hadn't taken that plane," or, "If only he hadn't decided to go to that store and gotten robbed." Many mourners are overcome with guilt for the smallest of coincidences—for example, if the person was hit by a car while buying you something, or if you worry that you didn't say the right thing the last time you saw him or her. People have to overcome the shock of not seeing the person again before they can start feeling the loss and understanding how he or she will never return.

An officer of the New York Police Department was killed while on duty, and he left behind a wife and four daughters. Here, mourners follow his flag-draped coffin. An unexpected death leaves loved ones trying to overcome the shock of the sudden tragedy.

People often worry that they didn't say the right thing to the person the last time they were together. But remember—the last interaction you have with someone isn't that important. People expect their lives and relationships to be ongoing. They expect that they will have time to have fights—and make up. They expect that they'll have more time to explain something. It would be very unnatural to live life as if you expected that every time you left someone you loved, you would never see that person again. To live in constant fear of death is to deny life.

SUICIDE IS A SPECIAL CASE

Many people feel particularly guilty if someone they love commits suicide. They wonder what they could have done to stop it. Although it is important to pass along information to trusted adults if you suspect a friend is suicidal, nobody knows for certain what is in another person's mind. Many times, suicidal people are crippled with depression. It doesn't matter how good their lives were or how much they were loved because something, possibly chemical, was happening in their brains that wasn't telling them the truth. It was making them feel worthless and hopeless.

Teens may be worried that they'll be tempted to commit suicide, too. But the great majority of people who have a loved one who commits suicide do not follow in that person's footsteps, no matter how challenging life gets.

MILITARY DEATHS

It can be very painful to have a loved one die in a war. But according to CNN, more than 7,000 coalition soldiers

Family and friends attend a graveside service for a U.S. Marine lance corporal who was killed fighting in the war in Afghanistan. Fellow marines begin to fold the flag that drapes the officer's casket to present it to his family.

have been killed as a result of the wars in Iraq and Afghanistan. Roughly 5,000 children have lost a parent, and more than 5,200 have lost a sibling, according to estimates. This kind of loss can be very difficult for survivors. One of the special things is that many people who aren't involved in military life don't understand what it's like to have a parent, brother, or sister far away and in constant danger, and then what it's like to lose him or her.

"I hate it when people find out about my dad and they say, 'I'm sorry.' You want to ask, 'Why are you sorry?'" said sixteen-year-old Wes Greene of Branford, Connecticut, whose soldier father was killed in Iraq in 2004. He told CNN what he would rather hear is, "Thank you for your father's sacrifice."

CHAPTER 5

How You Can Help Yourself

Some experts believe that one good way to heal from grief is to know when to put grieving aside to live daily life. There are many active ways to help heal suffering. They include creative, social, exercise, and other outlets. Marietta, age sixteen, was very sad when she lost her uncle to suicide. But instead of avoiding life and just grieving, she decided to lose extra weight and become an A student, for instance. For her, making a new commitment to her own goals was a way to honor her uncle. Are there any goals that you've been putting off? Like Marietta, you might find grieving to be a good time to start making a list of things that you care about achieving in your life. You can also find relief from sadness by taking actions to help yourself.

SELF-CARE

For some people, one of the hardest things to do when they're grieving is to handle the small, everyday routines of life. Pay special attention to simple things. Take a shower. Change your clothes. Brush your hair. Eat healthy food at regular mealtimes. Go to sleep at a customary time. You may even want to make a chart to help yourself

When you are trying to cope with grief, it's particularly important to make sure that you eat right. Learning to cook healthful food is a skill that you can use for life.

remember. As New Jersey therapist Cathy Gilio told the author, although these routines may not make you feel better right away, "at least you won't fall behind." On a hard day, these can be accomplishments that you can take pride in.

EXERCISE AND SUNLIGHT

Author Ruth Davis Konigsberg told the *Huffington Post* that if there's one thing that can help improve a grieving person's mood it is, "Exercise, hands down . . . It's the best anti-depressant there is" exercise—even taking a simple half-hour walk every day—can bring chemicals called endorphins rushing into your brain, which boost your mood. It can be natural to be angry or upset at the unfairness of losing someone. Exercise can help you feel less angry. Some people do better with aggressive exercise, like team sports or running, others with gentler forms such as tai chi, yoga, or taking walks. According to Konigsberg, "It can be natural to carry some of the suffering you feel around in your body. One of the other benefits of exercise is that it can release some of that pain." It can help you get your mind and body focused on living in the moment. It can also help you reach goals that will make you proud of yourself.

Getting outside can be important, too. Every day you exercise, even for a short time, you can take pride in it. The Japanese have a word for it—*Shinrin-yoku*, or "forest bathing." Being outside, especially around trees or other natural landscapes, can help reconnect you to the natural world and reduce sadness.

ART

Many people find it comforting to express themselves in art. The freedom of molding cool, moist clay into any shape you want can be satisfying when you're sad. Taking

Expressing your creativity through art can let you explore your feelings without words.

a paintbrush and splashing bright reds and blues onto plain paper can put color back into a world that feels gray. Sometimes, it's more important to paint something that feels enjoyable—the movement of paint on the page—and let yourself go, rather than force yourself to try to imagine something concrete. Some people like to draw mandalas. A mandala is a circular pattern that starts from a center. Put a dot in the middle of a piece of paper. Then surround it with small patterns or words. This kind of rhythmic, concentrated work can have a soothing effect on your mind, and often, it is quite beautiful.

Making collages can be a great way of surprising yourself with what you are thinking. Cut out a bunch of images from magazines, throw them in a box, and when you are ready, start putting them together in ways that make sense to you. You can choose a theme ahead of time or let one emerge. Sometimes you can find yourself thinking new thoughts. Rebecca, age seventeen, was angry at her father for being an alcoholic before he died. He would yell and criticize her when he was drunk, and then not remember his harsh words the next day. This conduct left her feeling very confused about why she didn't miss him. But then she made a collage of his life. It turned out that the pictures she found to cut out that most reminded her of him showed a different side of him. In spite of his alcoholism, he was often very caring. He was also interested in many things she hadn't thought about, like camping. She remembered good times she had with him when they were camping. The collage made him seem alive as an individual in a new way.

"The Bustle in a House," Poem XXII
By Emily Dickinson

The bustle in a house
The morning after death
Is solemnest of industries
Enacted upon earth,—

The sweeping up the heart,
And putting love away
We shall not want to use again
Until eternity.

Source: Dickinson, Emily. *The Poems of Emily Dickinson: Series One*. Boston, MA: Roberts Brothers, 1896.

You can also make portraits or draw cartoon panels about the person you love that tell about memories. Why is it so satisfying to create art when you're feeling troubled? Dr. Rachel Naomi Remen, an expert on grief said, "At the deepest level, the creative process and the healing process arise from a single source. When you are an artist, you are a healer."

WRITING

Dr. James Pennebaker, a psychology professor at the University of Texas, assigns his students to write about something traumatic that happened to them for fifteen minutes each day. That's because he carried out a study that showed that students who had kept journals about their traumas, compared to students who just wrote

The act of writing about your loved one or friend can help release pain and keep precious memories alive.

about everyday events, improved greatly. "When people are given the opportunity to write about emotional upheavals, they often experience improved health," Pennebaker says. "They go to the doctor less. They have changes in immune function. If they are first-year college students, their grades tend to go up. People will tell us months afterward that it's been a very beneficial experience for them."

It's understandable why writing can help grievers. In a journal, you can express all of your contradictory feelings. You can also put down memories of your loved ones as they come to you. That way you can feel safe that you won't lose them. Another thing that you can do is start a dream journal, especially if you have dreams of the person you lost. If you hold on to your writings, you can see how your feelings change. But even if you destroy your writing right away, you will still get benefits, Pennebaker says. The act of writing alone is helpful.

DO SOMETHING FOR OTHERS

One way of moving beyond your pain is by helping others. Even a little bit can help. Alexandra "Alex" Scott was diagnosed with neuroblastoma, a kind of cancer, before she was one. At the age of four, she decided to start a lemonade stand to raise money for research for cancer. From that small beginning came the charity Alex's Lemonade Stand. Sadly, Alex died at the age of eight in 2004—but

Alex's Lemonade Stand is just one of the great charities that can use young people's assistance. Supporting others can help you honor the person you lost.

by that time, she at least knew that her charity had raised more than a million dollars. A huge number of kids and adults continued to start their own lemonade stands (and other fund-raisers) to support Alex's charity. Corporations have also helped. To date, Alex's Lemonade Stand has raised $55 million for cancer research and treatment. But it wouldn't have been possible without many individuals who did their small bit—"one cup at a time," as the charity says. You may not be able or ready to run a charity as a young person, but every charity needs volunteers of one sort or another. If your sister died of leukemia or your father was killed by a drunk driver, there are specific charities that help cut down on those kinds of deaths that you can support. As American poet Ralph Waldo Emerson once said, "It is one of the most beautiful compensations of life, that no man can sincerely try to help another without helping himself."

CHAPTER 6

Cybergrieving

Traditionally, deaths were announced in the newspaper, along with an obituary notice detailing the person's life and the location of the funeral. Close friends and family were also notified by phone. After the funeral, friends of the family would write thoughtful sympathy cards about what the person meant to them. Then the families would write back with thanks for the cards. These rituals took place over days and weeks and gave dignity to the loss of a loved one.

Now, however, when everyone can share what they are eating, doing, and thinking on the Internet in an instant, news of a death is likely to travel instantly over the Internet as well. People send out invitations to the funeral by e-mail, spread the word by Twitter, and comment on people's blogs, Web pages, and Facebook accounts. Many funeral homes offer online guest books and memory pages for remembering loved ones and to help with the grieving process. Media companies, such as

Webcasting Funerals

Some funeral homes are starting to offer two-way Webcasting. That allows people who are unable to be at a funeral to link to a special Web site and watch the service from wherever they are. In an era when so many families in the United States and Canada have international members, this can help viewers feel as if they have not missed out. It can help people who are too old or ill to see the funeral as well. Funeral homes can help set up a way to allow these mourners to share their memories of the person who died in real time at appropriate moments. Then the funeral home can make a DVD of the funeral so that the family can keep those memories.

Legacy.com, offer readers online obituaries, death notices, and links to grief support groups.

WHEN CYBERCOMMUNICATION GOES BAD

In 2010, fifteen-year-old Phoebe Prince killed herself in South Hadley, Massachusetts, after being bullied. After her death, she was still being victimized—in cyberspace. According to *Boston Magazine*, a "We Murdered Phoebe Prince" page appeared on Facebook, her picture changed so it looked as if knives were being stuck into her eyes. When Phoebe committed suicide, some people left cruel messages for her parents to read. One was "she deserved

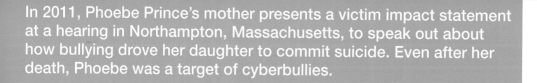

In 2011, Phoebe Prince's mother presents a victim impact statement at a hearing in Northampton, Massachusetts, to speak out about how bullying drove her daughter to commit suicide. Even after her death, Phoebe was a target of cyberbullies.

it." One of the coldest was a single word. "Accomplished."

FACEBOOK AND DEATH

Facebook eventually took down Phoebe Prince's personal page, but what normally happens to someone who has died and has a Facebook page? It's an important issue. According to Technorati.com, as of March 2012, there were more than thirty million accounts on Facebook of people who had died. What happens currently is that Facebook has a special process for memorializing the dead. Basically, it locks the account of the person who died. The only people who are allowed to ask for the site to be taken down are family members. The only people who are allowed to still comment on the page are friends and family who made comments before the death was reported. But that is only if Facebook is told of the death.

THE KINDER SIDE OF CYBERGRIEVING

In Rancho Santa Margarita, California, a group of 150 teens gathered at the street corner where a classmate, Taylor Sams, died in a car crash early on a Sunday morning in September 2011. They were holding a candlelight ceremony to remember her. Her friend Bernardo Medeiros announced the gathering on Facebook on Sunday afternoon, and by that night, the mourners gathered at the corner. Posters with her picture were taped to trees, and grieving friends lit candles to remember her life. Another campaign suggesting people wear white in her honor was announced on Facebook that same day. Madeiros told the *Rancho Santa Margarita Patch* that he and Taylor had made plans to hang out over the summer, but it hadn't happened. "It's crazy to think about how fast your life can come and go," he said.

WHAT ARE SOME GOOD GUIDELINES FOR USING THE INTERNET?

If a death is announced by a friend on Facebook, you can briefly offer your condolences right away, but also, start preparing a more thought-out message to send either by card (which is more proper) through the mail or as a private e-mail to the mourners. It doesn't need to be long, but it would be nice for a message or note to have the following elements:

1. Sympathy for the family's loss.
2. Some kind memory of the person who died.
3. A sentence to support the person you're writing to.
4. Proper language with no abbreviations.

The family that is mourning traditionally answers the letters they receive. They thank people who helped at the funeral, but they also write letters to thank people for remembering their loved one. This acknowledgment can be done on or offline. Although it is painful, it can also be a reminder of a special connection.

In the weeks ahead, don't forget to check in, even in little ways, with the mourners. In addition, don't forget that face time can be better than Facebook time to suffering friends and family members.

HOW THE INTERNET CAN HELP

One of the more positive aspects of the Internet is that it can build connections and communities. Because young people are often more technology savvy than many older ones, they can make a special contribution to help in keeping the memory of someone special who died alive. Many are making Facebook pages, the way Bernardo Madeiros did, or sending out Twitter feeds, texts, or e-mails to urge people to take a certain action—such as gathering together or even doing something charitable as a group in the deceased person's name.

Sometimes keeping or maintaining a Web site or Facebook page about a loved one can let you connect with other people who cared for the person you lost.

Volunteering to host a family blog is something that could be very much appreciated. People can write stories, post pictures, or write poems that express their feelings and share them. Scanning in photos, making sure that the memories are respectful, and understanding how open or private the blog should be are things that younger people often have a better grasp of. It would also give you a chance to connect with other people who loved your friend or relative.

An advantage of making a blog or Web page for a loved one is that you can add special features that help others. For example, you can add a donation Web site for the National Cancer Society if your loved one died of cancer. You can also include Web resources that help people with grief.

Technology is undoubtedly changing the face of how people communicate about grief in the modern world. But as long as people love and die, the emotions that surround death—both bitter and sweet—will remain.

GLOSSARY

AMYGDALA A part of the brain involved in strong emotions.

BEREAVEMENT The state of grieving.

CASKET A special kind of box in which dead people are buried.

CLERGYPERSON A person who performs services as a religious leader.

COMPLICATED GRIEF A form of grieving that is intense and prolonged.

CREMATION The burning of human remains instead of burial.

DEPRESSION A sense of unrelenting sadness or grayness that can last for long periods and that may require medical help.

FUNERAL A service for someone who died, usually with the coffin present.

GRIEF A feeling of intense sorrow and loss.

LEUKEMIA A cancer of the white blood cells, which are also referred to as leukocytes.

MANDALA A circular pattern that starts from a center.

MEMORIAL A service at which someone who died is remembered.

MOURNING Another word for the suffering caused by another's death.

NEUROBLASTOMA A kind of nerve cancer most commonly found in children.

PERVADE Be present and apparent throughout.

RECONCILE Have two different things make sense together.

RESILIENCE An ability to adapt to difficult circumstances and thrive.

RUMINATION Repeating and obsessive thoughts, usually unpleasant.

SERMON A speech delivered by a clergyperson.

SHINRIN-YOKU "Forest bathing," or spending time out in nature, especially in the woods.

TRANSITION A state of change or alteration.

WAKE A time before a funeral where people gather beside the body of a loved one.

FOR MORE INFORMATION

Alex's Lemonade Stand Foundation (ALSF)
333 East Lancaster Avenue, #414
Wynnewood, PA 19096
(866) 333-1213
Web site: http://www.alexslemonade.org
Alex's Lemonade Stand Foundation started from the
lemonade stand of cancer patient Alex Scott, who
died in 2004. Now this multimillion-dollar charity
provides hope for other childhood cancer patients. It
helps individuals and families with children who have
cancer and funds cancer research. It welcomes and
supports fund-raising efforts—including lemonade
stands—by young people.

American Foundation for Suicide Prevention
120 Wall Street, 29th Floor
New York, NY 10005
(888) 333-AFSP (2377) or (212) 363-3500
Web site: http://www.afsp.org
This foundation provides online resources and research
on suicide and suicide prevention. If you are in crisis,
please call the National Suicide Prevention Lifeline
at (800) 273-TALK (8255).

Canadian Association for Suicide Prevention
870 Portage Avenue
Winnipeg, MB R3G 0P1
Canada
Web site: http://www.suicideprevention.ca

The Canadian Association for Suicide Prevention has an extensive list of articles about suicide risk, lists crisis centers across the country for those at risk, supports World Suicide Prevention Day, and provides survivor support as well.

Centers for Disease Control and Prevention (CDC)
Division of Adolescent and School Health
4770 Buford Highway NE MS K29
Atlanta, GA 30341
(800) CDC-INFO [232-4636]
Web site: http://www.cdc.gov/healthyyouth
This government resource provides extensive information about aspects of health that affect young people's lifespans, including details about violence, suicide, and disease. It also gives statistical information on disease and causes of death.

Compassionate Friends
900 Jorie Boulevard, Suite 78
Oak Brook, IL 60523
(877) 969-0010
Web site: http://www.compassionatefriends.org
This organization was founded mainly to support families after a child dies. It has meetings for parents and meetings, brochures, and other materials for grieving siblings. It also hosts special events, such as a worldwide candle lighting in honor of the dead.

The Dougy Center: The National Center for Grieving
    Children and Families
3903 SE 52nd Avenue
Portland, OR 97206
(866) 775-5683
Web site: http://www.dougy.org
The Dougy Center provides local resources in Portland,
    but also provides information about how to cope with
    suicide loss and a hotline for people at risk of sui-
    cide. The Web site includes a list of recommended
    books. The group also offers national resources for
    adults, kids, teens, and young adults, including the
    bill of rights for grieving teens and a finder for more
    than five hundred grief support centers around the
    United States.

National Alliance of Grieving Children
P.O. Box 2373
Stuart, FL 34995
(866) 432-1542
Web site: http://childrengrieve.org
The National Alliance for Grieving Children lists grief
    support providers and groups that serve kids, teens
    and their families. It provides information about where
    to find help and surveys on children and grieving, and
    helps support Children's Grief Awareness Day.

Rainbows Canada
Suite 545, 80 Bradford Street

Barrie, ON L4N 6S7
Canada
(877) 403-2733
Web site: http://www.rainbows.ca
Rainbows for All Children Canada's motto is "Guiding Kids Through Life Storms." It is dedicated to helping children and teens grieve and grow after loss, both through death and divorce. It helps establish grief support groups all over Canada for vulnerable kids and teens.

WEB SITES

Due to the changing nature of Internet links, Rosen Publishing has developed an online list of Web sites related to the subject of this book. This site is updated regularly. Please use this link to access the list:

http://www.rosenlinks.com/HELP/Grief

FOR FURTHER READING

Albom, Mitch. *Tuesdays with Morrie: An Old Man, a Young Man, and Life's Greatest Lesson*. New York, NY: Random House, 2007.

Alcott, Louisa May. *Little Women*. Gregory Eiselein and Anne K. Phillips, eds. New York, NY: Norton Critical Editions, 2003.

Bonanno, George A. *The Other Side of Sadness: What the New Science of Bereavement Tells Us About Life After Loss*. New York, NY: Basic Books, 2009.

Brezina, Corona. *FAQ: Frequently Asked Questions About When a Friend Dies*. New York, NY: Rosen Publishing, 2008.

Ciarrochi, Joseph, Louise Hayes, Ann Bailey, and Steven Hayes. *Get Out of Your Mind and into Your Life for Teens*. Oakland, CA: New Harbinger Publications, 2012.

Cook, Colleen Ryckert. *FAQ: Frequently Asked Questions About Cancer Decisions for You and Your Family*. New York, NY: Rosen Publishing, 2011.

Cook, Colleen Ryckert. *FAQ: Frequently Asked Questions About Social Networking*. New York, NY: Rosen Publishing, 2011.

Furgang, Kathy. *Netiquette: A Student's Guide to Digital Etiquette*. New York, NY: Rosen Publishing, 2010.

Giddens, Sandra. *FAQ: Frequently Asked Questions About Suicide*. New York, NY: Rosen Publishing, 2009.

Gray, Keith. *Ostrich Boys.* New York, NY: Random House Books for Young Readers, 2010.

Green, John. *The Fault in Our Stars*. New York, NY: Dutton Juvenile, 2012.

Hart, Joyce. *FAQ: Frequently Asked Questions About Being Part of a Military Family*. New York, NY: Rosen Publishing, 2009.

Henningfeld, Diana Andrews. *Death and Dying* (Global Viewpoints). Farmington Hills, MI: Greenhaven Press, 2010.

Huddle, Lorena, and Jay Schleifer. *Teen Suicide*. New York, NY: Rosen Publishing, 2012.

Kornfeld, Jody, Sophie Waters, and Kathy Furgang. *Death and Bereavement*. New York, NY: Rosen Publishing, 2010.

Levin, Judith. *Depression and Mood Disorders*. New York, NY: Rosen Publishing, 2008.

Pausch, Randy, with Jeffrey Zaslow. *The Last Lecture*. New York, NY: Hyperion, 2008.

Ryan, Darlene. *Five Minutes More*. Custer, WA: Orca Book Publishers, 2009.

Shannon, Chelsey. *Chelsey: My True Story of Murder, Loss, and Starting Over*. Deerfield Beach, FL: Health Communications, 2009.

Van Dijk, Sheri. *Don't Let Your Emotions Run Your Life for Teens.* Oakland, CA: New Harbinger Publications, 2011.

Vincent, Erin. *Grief Girl: My True Story*. New York, NY: Random House, 2008.

Ware, Bronnie. *The Top Five Regrets of the Dying: A Life Transformed by the Dearly Departing*. New York, NY: Hay House, 2012.

Wolfelt, Alan D. *Finding Hope and Healing Your Heart*. Fort Collins, CO: Companion Press. 2009.

Wolfelt, Alan D. *Healing Your Grieving Body: 100 Physical Practices for Mourners*. Fort Collins, CO: Companion Press, 2009.

Wolfelt, Alan D. *Understanding Your Suicide Grief: Ten Essential Touchstones for Finding Hope and Healing Your Heart*. Fort Collins, CO: Companion Press, 2009.

BIBLIOGRAPHY

ABC Primetime. "Charlize Theron's Family Tragedy."
ABCnews.com. Retrieved August 10, 2012 (http://
www. abcnews.go.com/Primetime).

Beretsky, Summer. "How Facebook Changes the Way
We Mourn Death." PsychCentral.com (Parts 1–4).
Retrieved October 2012 (http://blogs.psychcentral.
com/panic/2012/10/how-facebook-changes-the
-way-we-mourn-death).

Biography.com. "Madonna. Biography." A+E Television
Networks, LLC. Retrieved October 1, 2012 (http://
www.biography.com/people/madonna-9394994).

Biography.com. "Synopsis: Rosie O'Donnell." A+E
Television Networks, LLC. Retrieved October 11, 2012
(http://www.biography.com/people/rosie-odonnell
-9542144).

"Breaking Night: Liz Murray's Journey from Darkness to
Light." *Teen Voices*, Vol. 20, Issue 1, Spring/Summer
2011, pp. 24–25.

Canfield, Jack, et al. *Chicken Soup for the Soul: Just for
Teenagers*. New York, NY: Simon and Schuster, 2011.

Canfield, Jack, et al. *Chicken Soup for the Soul: Tough Times
for Teens*. New York, NY: Simon and Schuster, 2012.

Carter, Chelsea J. "A Weekend at Grief Camp: 'It's Never
Going to Be the Same.'" CNN.com, June 11, 2012.
Retrieved October 18, 2012 (http://www.cnn.com
/2012/06/10/us/grief-camp-military-teens/index.html).

deVita-Raeburn, Elizabeth. *The Empty Room: Surviving
the Loss of a Brother or Sister at Any Age*. New York,
NY: Scribner, 2004.

Dickinson, Emily. *The Poems of Emily Dickinson: Series One*. Boston, MA: Roberts Brothers, 1896.

Gaines, Jordan. "Turning Trauma into Story: The Benefits of Journaling." *Psychology Today*, August 17, 2012. Retrieved October 18, 2012 (http://www .psychologytoday.com/blog/brain-babble/201208 /turning-trauma-story-the-benefits-journaling).

Giacobbe, Alyssa. "Who Failed Phoebe Prince?" *Boston Magazine*, June 2010. Retrieved October 17, 2012 (http://www.bostonmagazine.com/articles/2010/05 /phoebe-prince).

Hochman, David. "Jon Hamm: 'I Stopped Believing in a Storybook Existence a Long Time Ago.'" *Parade*, July 28, 2010. Retrieved September 7, 2012 (http:/www .parade.com/celebrity/celebrity-parade/2010/jon -hamm-mad-men.html).

Konigsberg, Ruth Davis. *The Truth About Grief: The Myth of Its Five Stages and the New Science of Loss*. New York, NY: Simon and Schuster, 2011.

Kubler-Ross, Elizabeth. *On Death and Dying*. New York, NY: Touchstone, 1969.

Ma, Lybi. "Good Grief: Coping After Loss." *Psychology Today*, May 1, 2003. Retrieved September 1, 2012 (http://www.psychologytoday.com/articles/200303 /good-grief-coping-after-loss).

Murphy, Sherry L., Jiaquan Xu, and Kenneth Kochanek. "Deaths: Preliminary Data for 2010." National Vital Statistics Reports Centers for Disease Control,

January 11, 2012. Retrieved October 18, 2012 (http://www.cdc.gov/nchs/data/nvsr/nvsr60/nvsr60_04.pdf).

"My Dad Is My Guardian Angel." *M Magazine*. Volume 12, Issue 6, June 12, 2012, pp. 42, 43.

Petrecca, Laura. "Mourning Becomes Electric: Tech Changes the Way We Grieve." *USA Today*, June 30, 2012. Retrieved October 18, 2012 (http://usatoday30.usatoday.com/money/industries/technology/story/2012-05-07/digital-mourning/55268806/1).

Rancho Santa Margarita Patch. "UPDATE: Crash Kills 18-Year-Old." September 18, 2011. Retrieved October 2012 (http://ranchosantamargarita.patch.com/articles/rollover-on-241-kills-woman).

Schuurman, Donna. *Never the Same: Coming to Terms with the Death of a Parent*. New York, NY: St. Martin's Press, 2003.

Sturt, Kristen. "8 Famous People Raised by Grandparents: Grandparents Didn't Just Raise These Celebrities—They Gave Them the Tools to Succeed." Retrieved September 12, 2012 (http://www.grandparents.com/food-and-leisure/celebrity/famous-people-raised-grandparents).

Washburn, Lindy, and Barbara Williams. "For Families That Lose a Child, 'A Part of You Dies.'" *The Record*, May 25, 2012. Retrieved October 17, 2012 (http://www.northjersey.com/cliffsidepark/052512_For_families_that_lose_a_child__a_part_of_you_dies_.html?page=all).

INDEX

ABOUT THE AUTHOR

New Jersey author Alexandra Hanson-Harding has watched her young sons cope with the loss of three of their beloved grandparents. It is through watching their struggles to make meaning of those deaths that grief has been made a meaningful subject to her. As the writer of sixteen books on such subjects as physical bullying and helping girls to be advocates for other young women, she has a strong belief that teenagers can suffer deep pain, yet have the resilience, empathy, and courage to use their experiences to make good lives for themselves and others.

PHOTO CREDITS